AI v/s Spirituality

Spirituality - A Way of Life

Rishikesh Upadhyay

notionpress.com

INDIA • SINGAPORE • MALAYSIA

ISBN
Paperback 979-8-90479-138-4
Hardcase 979-8-90479-139-1

Contents

Disclaimer

I have tried to present Learnings and Knowledge acquired during my life and observing journey of many spiritual gurus. I have also learnt from the Autobiography of our ancient spiritual personalities.

I am regularly practicing mind-fulness so well aware about its benefits in life and its effect on Health and Wellness. I also took other's opinion and tried to include their views.

This book should not be used as a substitute for the advice of a competent Spiritual Gurus. They have vast knowledge and guide us in every aspect of life.

Acknowledgement

First and foremost, praises and thanks to the God, the Almighty, for his showers of blessings throughout my work.

I am truly grateful for the guidance provided by the Spiritual Gurus of Swaminarayan, Brahmakumaris, Art of Living and others. On this occasion, I am grateful for all my Vipassana teachers and their guidance. I am also thankful to the deep thinkers and readers of Sri Ramkrishna Mission.

I also learnt from the life of Sri Vivekananda at very early age.

My sincere pranam to my late mother ***Mrs. Aruna Manuprasad Upadhyay,*** who gave inclination for Lord Sri Krishna and imbibed respect towards other religions.

I extend gratitude to all my friends, who helped me by giving an opportunity to learn about their religion and the learnings from their experienced persons and devotees. I am grateful for their valuable advice, constructive feedback, positive appreciation throughout the journey.

I sincerely thank my wife **Mrs. Manisha** and Children **Miss Jalak** and **Master Dev** for their valuable suggestions.

My heartfelt regard goes to my father for his unconditional love and moral support.

Dedication

I dedicate this book to my father in-law late ***Mr. Vishwanath L. Jani***, who used to worship Shankar (Mahadev / Bholanath) and his routine business life started after worshiping Mahakaleswar Mandir – Una. After retirement from the business, he used to spend more than 2 hours in Mahadev Puja.

I learnt from the life of various spiritual gurus, who imbibed spirituality at very early age in my life. I understood the true sense of spirituality. It is a connection to something larger than oneself and translating all deeds, which provide purpose in life. It also spreads peace, purpose, and connection with others. I realized that true personal growth happens only when the person mingles with nature, art and doing something creative and involved in his/her hobby.

I learnt from my father that spirituality is a way of life living beyond selfless. I must thank him for his untiring guidance and support in all kind of up and down in life.

Abstract

1.0 Introduction

AI and human creativity are two forces that, while distinct, can complement and enhance each other in powerful ways. Here's an exploration of how they relate:

1. Human Creativity

   Human creativity is typically associated with the ability to imagine, innovate, and produce new ideas, concepts, or artifacts. It is influenced by a combination of factors:

   - Emotions and experiences: Our personal history, culture, and emotional responses play a significant role in shaping creative output.
   - Intuition and imagination: Humans can make leaps of logic, think abstractly, and draw connections between seemingly unrelated ideas.
   - Purpose and meaning: Many creative endeavors are driven by a sense of purpose, a desire to express oneself, or to communicate complex human experiences.

2.0 AI and Creativity

Artificial intelligence (AI) is increasingly being used to assist, augment, and even generate creative work. AI systems can analyze vast datasets, learn patterns, and generate outputs that mimic or complement human creativity. Some examples include:

- Generative art: AI can produce paintings, music, poetry, and even video game worlds. Algorithms like GANs (Generative Adversarial Networks) or transformer models (like GPT) have been used to create works that resemble those made by human artists.
- Design assistance: AI tools are used to help designers with tasks like generating patterns, layouts, or even suggesting product designs based on user preferences.
- Music composition: AI can compose music in various genres, analyzing historical pieces and generating novel melodies, harmonies, and rhythms.
- Writing: Language models, like GPT, assist in writing stories, scripts, or articles by suggesting ideas, completing sentences, or drafting entire works.

3.0 How AI and Human Creativity Intersect

AI isn't replacing human creativity but can enhance it in several ways:

- Augmentation: AI tools can serve as a collaborator, allowing humans to explore ideas more quickly, providing inspiration, and giving suggestions that a human may not have considered.
- Exploration: AI can process vast amounts of data to suggest new possibilities, uncover hidden patterns, or even create hybrid forms of art that wouldn't otherwise occur.
- Breaking barriers: AI can assist in fields where human creativity may be limited by time, space, or skill. For example, AI can help create complex visual effects in films or design intricate architectural structures that are then fine-tuned by human experts.

- Automation: Some routine or repetitive creative tasks, such as generating variations of designs or composing simple music, can be automated by AI, freeing up humans to focus on higher-level creative decision-making.

4.0 Limitations of AI in Creativity

While AI can produce impressive outputs, there are still significant differences between human and machine creativity:

- Lack of emotional depth: AI does not experience emotions or understand the human condition in the way that humans do. Its creations lack the emotional nuances and intentionality that often characterize human art.
- Context and meaning: AI can analyze data but does not inherently understand the context, history, or culture behind its creations. It lacks a true sense of meaning or purpose.
- Originality: While AI can generate new combinations based on existing data, it lacks the "original" spark of creativity that often involves thinking beyond existing patterns, challenging norms, and inventing new paradigms.

5.0 Collaborative Potential

The true potential of AI and human creativity lies in collaboration. AI can handle repetitive tasks, process vast amounts of data, and suggest novel approaches, while humans can bring emotional depth, intuition, and conceptual thinking. In fields like art, literature, music, and design, this partnership can push the boundaries of what is possible.

For example:

- Artists may use AI tools to help create intricate visuals but still bring their own perspectives and artistic choices to the final piece.

- Writers may use AI for idea generation, but human judgment will guide the final narrative arc, ensuring emotional resonance and meaningful themes.
- Musicians may collaborate with AI to generate melodies or harmonies, but the human touch remains essential in crafting the final composition's feel and structure.

6.0 Conclusion

AI and human creativity are not opposing forces but complementary ones. While AI can assist and inspire, it is the unique qualities of human creativity — intuition, emotion, and the ability to find deep meaning — that continue to shape the world in profound and unpredictable ways. The future likely holds exciting opportunities for synergy, where human artists, designers, writers, and creators of all kinds can leverage AI to enhance their work, explore new ideas, and push the boundaries of what is possible.

References

1. No specific single source

1

Introduction of AI

1.0 Introduction

Artificial Intelligence (AI) is a latest technology that facilitate machine to utilise technologies so that it can replicate human creative skills including capabilities to complete the tasks require to do learning, reasoning creation and making decisions.

2.0 Elements

The main elements of AI

1. ***Machine Learning (ML)***

   It is a part of AI, in which algorithms set such that it can improve performance over time by learning from past records, historical data, and other supervised, unsupervised tasks. This will also have learning capabilities.

2. ***Natural Language Processing (NLP)***

   Enables machines to understand, interpret, and generate human language, thereby supporting applications like chatbots, translation tools, and speech recognition systems.

3. ***Computer Vision***

   It helps machines to understand visual data, as provided in facial identity and object personalization.

4. ***Robotics***

   It uses Artificial Intelligence of any machines to perform tasks without intervene of man or any external entity an take decision based on data provided or set previously and act such as autonomous vehicles and prosthetic limbs.

5. ***Expert Systems***

   It takes decision and carries out the processes by way of establishing sequence of operation and guidance set through specialized areas, entering rules and general details.

6. ***Reinforcement Learning***

   It empowers systems to consider choices based on various inputs and other variables received from external environment.

   AI is used in all the industries and almost every business that includes healthcare, finance, entertainment, vehicle driving, taking smart decision and critical problem-solving areas. It also raises ethical questions around privacy, bias, and societal impact.

2.0 Difference between AI and ML

AI is a whole concept that includes the system that resonant human intelligence, while ML is a branch /subset of AI that concentrate on learning from past record or history / similar data set previously. In general, AI as the umbrella whereas ML is a subset having deep learning, robotics, and NLP.

3.0 Applications of AI and ML

AI and ML are business transformation by automating processes, improving decision-making, and enhancing experiences:

- ***Healthcare***

  Patient monitoring, diagnostics, research & development of new drugs, and predictive analytics.

- ***Manufacturing***

  It helps in predictive maintenance and improves operational efficiency, and IoT analytics.

- ***Retail and Ecommerce***

  It gives personalized recommendations, demand forecasting, and also helps in optimization of supply chain activities.

- ***Finance***

  Fraud detection, risk analysis, and automated trading.

- ***Telecommunications***

  Network optimization, business automation, and capacity planning.

4.0 Natural Language Processing (NLP)

NLP allows machines to understand and carry out process similar to human language using methods like machine learning, neural networks, and text mining.

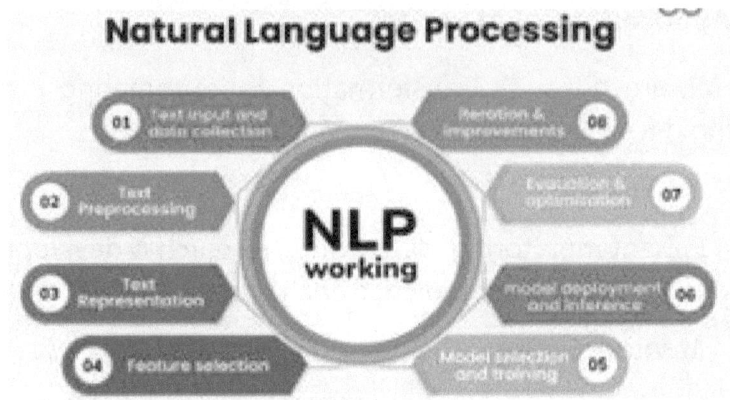

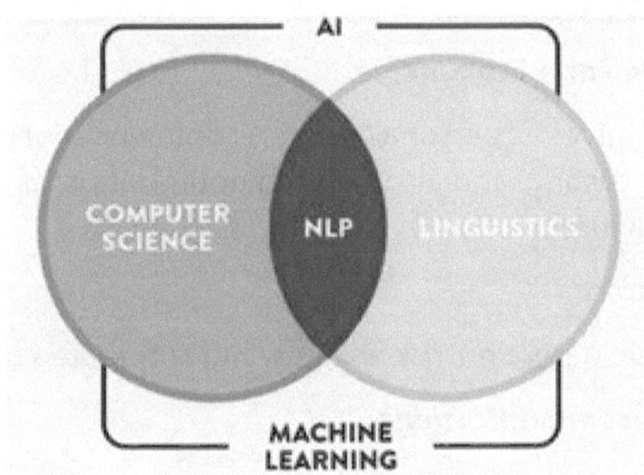

Applications include:

- Virtual assistants like Siri and Alexa.
- Email spam filtering and grammar checking.
- Automatic translation and document summarization.
- Sentiment analysis and market prediction.
- By blending computer science, linguistics, and AI, NLP enhances how systems interact with human language.

References

1. No specific single source

2

Intelligence in a Global Context

1.0 Global Intelligence

In a global context, Artificial Intelligence has capabilities to carry out processes like human and take decision based on various data available from an environment and solve problems, make decisions, and adjust to the complexities of global systems.

2.0 Different types of Intelligence

General Indication of following diverse intelligence given below.

1. **Human Intelligence**

   Human intelligence on a global scale is shaped by cultural, social, and environmental factors:

   - ***Cognitive Diversity***

     Cultures emphasize different forms of intelligence, including analytical, emotional, social, and creative capabilities.

   - ***Education Systems***

     Global priorities vary, from literacy and STEM education to fostering critical thinking, influencing intellectual development worldwide.

- ***Interdisciplinary Collaboration***

  Tackling global challenges requires integrated approaches, blending insights from fields like economics, science, sociology, and technology.

2. **Artificial Intelligence (AI)**

   AI plays a transformative role in global intelligence systems

- ***Applications Across Sectors***

  AI is revolutionizing industries such as healthcare, finance, education, and defense, driving efficiency and innovation globally.

- ***Geopolitical Stakes***

  Nations heavily invest in AI for economic growth and strategic military advantages, fueling a global AI race.

- ***Ethical Concerns***

  Issues like bias, surveillance, and data privacy prompt international discussions and initiatives to establish responsible AI frameworks.

3. **Economic Intelligence**

   Economic intelligence focuses on understanding and navigating global markets

- ***Corporate Strategy***

  Multinational corporations rely on market intelligence to stay competitive and adapt to global trends.

- ***National Security***

  Governments analyze economic data to inform trade policies and maintain stability.

- ***Technological Advancements***

  AI and big data are reshaping economic intelligence, offering insights into consumer behavior and optimizing supply chains.

4. **Political and Military Intelligence**

   These forms of intelligence are pivotal for global security and diplomacy

- **Surveillance and Espionage**

  Monitoring international relations, terrorism, and cybersecurity threats remains a priority for intelligence agencies.

- **Global Collaboration**

  Alliances like NATO depend on shared intelligence to make coordinated strategic decisions.

- ***Technological Innovation***

  Cyber warfare and satellite reconnaissance are redefining intelligence operations and military strategies.

5. **Environmental and Social Intelligence**

   Addressing global challenges like climate change and inequality requires adaptive intelligence:

- ***Climate Modeling***

  AI and big data help predict environmental trends and manage natural disasters.

- ***Social Policy***

  Analyzing issues like migration, health crises, and education systems demands a combination of social intelligence and global cooperation.

- ***Collective Governance***

  Organizations like the UN and WHO leverage collaborative intelligence to tackle transnational issues.

3.0 Challenges to Global Intelligence

Despite its potential, global intelligence faces several obstacles:

- ***Bias and Inequality***

  Intelligence systems often reflect systemic biases, favoring dominant nations or groups.

- ***Ethical Dilemmas***

  Questions about privacy, surveillance, and data ownership remain unresolved.

- ***Collaboration vs. Competition***

  Balancing national interests with global cooperation continues to pose challenges.

In today's interconnected world, intelligence is a cornerstone of innovation, decision-making, and problem-solving. To harness its full potential, ethical frameworks, interdisciplinary efforts, and global collaboration are essential to minimize risks and ensure equitable benefits.

References

1. No specific single source

3
Unreal World

1.0 Explain Unreal

The term *"unreal"* has varied meanings depending on the context:

1. ***Lacking Reality***

   Something artificial, not genuine, or illusory.

   Example: "The whole bizarre evening had an unreal quality to it."

2. ***Incredible***

   Something extremely good or surprising.

   Example: "We saw so many shooting stars that night, it was unreal!"

3. ***Imaginary***

   Describing something dreamlike, strange, or as if imagined.

   Example: "We just ate and ate, and I was so full it was unreal."

Additionally, *"Unreal"* refers to **Unreal Engine**, a powerful 3D creation tool widely used in game development, film, animation, and artificial intelligence (AI) applications.

2.0 Unreal Engine Overview

Key Features

- Known for its high-quality graphics, Unreal Engine creates immersive virtual worlds.
- Used for game development, simulations, and creative projects like films and animations.
- Includes **Verse**, a scripting language first implemented in *Fortnite*.
- Supported by **Fab**, a marketplace for buying, selling, and sharing digital assets.

3.0 Unreal Engine and Artificial Intelligence (AI)

Unreal Engine integrates AI tools for building virtual characters, training real-world AI systems, and powering advanced simulations:

1. **AI Tools for Building Virtual Characters**
   - **Behavior Trees**

     Manage decision-making for AI characters.
   - **Environment Query System (EQS)**

     Handles environmental queries to inform AI behavior.
   - **AI Perception**

     Simulates sensory inputs like sight and sound.
   - **Smart Objects**

     Enable interaction between AI agents and the game environment.
   - **Dynamic Decision-Making**

     Supports AI systems like Utility AI, where characters evaluate options and choose the best action.

- **Learning AI**

  Incorporates machine learning models that allow characters to adapt based on player actions.

2. **Training and Validating Real-World AI**

   Unreal Engine provides tools for developing and refining AI for non-gaming purposes:

   - Building simulation pipelines to test AI in virtual environments.
   - Capturing and replicating real-world data, such as city street layouts, for training self-driving cars.
   - Powering AI algorithms for robotics and industrial applications.

3. **Neural Network Engine (NNE):**

   Unreal Engine supports pre-trained neural network models, enabling tasks like

   - Animation and rendering.
   - Physics simulations.
   - AI-driven content generation.

4. **AI Image Generation**

   The engine can create sequences of images to visualize environments or storyboard ideas, aiding creative processes.

4.0 Impact of Unreal Engine AI on Industries

1. **Game Development**

   - Empowers developers with tools for procedural content generation, creating larger and more complex game worlds.
   - Features like MetaHumans and smart objects simplify the creation of detailed characters and assets.

2. **Efficiency Gains**
   - Enables the development of projects that previously required massive resources.
   - Democratizes access to advanced AI tools for indie developers and AAA studios alike.
3. **Cross-Industry Applications**
   - AI tools extend beyond gaming into robotics, virtual training environments, and real-world simulations.

5.0 Challenges of Using Unreal Engine AI

While Unreal Engine AI offers vast potential, it comes with unique challenges:

1. **Asset Size and Complexity:**
   - Modern games demand highly detailed worlds, with more characters, levels, and sophisticated materials.
   - Handling and storing these large assets requires advanced computing and storage infrastructure.
2. **Version Control Risks:**
   - Projects involving complex assets often generate multiple file versions, increasing the risk of data loss or overwriting.
3. **Resource Demands:**
   - Teams need robust tools and systems to manage the growing scale of projects efficiently.

6.0 Conclusion

Unreal Engine, with its advanced AI tools and high-quality graphics, continues to revolutionize industries from gaming to real-world AI applications. While its capabilities unlock new levels of creativity and efficiency, developers must address challenges like asset complexity and resource management to fully realize its potential.

References

1. https://sentencedict.com/bizarre.html

4

AI – Long Term Impact

1.0 Long-Term Impacts of Artificial Intelligence (AI)

Artificial Intelligence (AI) is reshaping industries, economies, and societies at an unprecedented pace. Its long-term impacts are multifaceted, with both significant benefits and potential challenges:

2.0 Potential Negative Impacts

1. **Job Displacement**

   - **Impact**

     AI can automate roles involving repetitive tasks, reducing the need for human labor, particularly in low-skilled jobs.

   - **Challenge**

     Reskilling and upskilling the workforce to adapt to new opportunities created by AI.

2. **Economic Inequality**

   - **Impact**

     Wealth and benefits of AI tend to concentrate among affluent individuals and corporations, widening the gap between rich and poor.

- **Challenge**

  Creating policies to distribute AI's economic gains equitably.

3. **Disinformation**

   - **Impact**

     Tools like deepfakes and AI-generated fake news can erode trust in media and social platforms.

   - **Challenge**

     Developing robust detection tools and fostering media literacy.

4. **Environmental Damage**

   - **Impact**

     AI systems, particularly large models, require massive computational power, contributing to significant energy consumption and carbon emissions.

   - **Challenge**

     Innovating energy-efficient AI technologies and adopting renewable energy sources.

5. **Ethical Dilemmas**

   - **Impact**

     AI raises complex questions about bias, transparency, privacy, and accountability.

   - **Challenge**

     Establishing ethical frameworks and governance mechanisms to address these concerns.

6. **Security Concerns**

   - **Impact**

     AI can amplify vulnerabilities in cybersecurity, enabling more sophisticated cyberattacks.

- **Challenge**

  Enhancing AI-driven defenses and risk management systems.

7. **Increased Regulation**

- **Impact**

  As AI becomes pervasive, governments will likely introduce stricter regulations to ensure its ethical and safe use.

- **Challenge**

  Balancing innovation with oversight to avoid stifling progress.

3.0 Potential Positive Impacts

1. **Economic Growth and Innovation**

- AI drives advancements across industries, from healthcare to finance, unlocking new efficiencies and opportunities.

2. **Improved Healthcare**

- AI enhances diagnostics, treatment personalization, and patient outcomes, addressing global health challenges.

3. **Enhanced Education**

- Personalized learning systems powered by AI can improve access to education and adapt to individual learning needs.

4. **Sustainability Solutions**

- AI aids in climate modeling, renewable energy optimization, and sustainable resource management.

5. **Increased Efficiency**

- Automation reduces errors, accelerates processes, and lowers costs in various industries.

6. **Global Problem-Solving**

   - AI facilitates solutions for transnational issues like pandemics, disaster response, and poverty alleviation.

4.0 AI Governance Frameworks

OECD Initiatives

The Organization for Economic Co-operation and Development (OECD) has developed comprehensive AI governance tools:

1. **AI Principles (2019, updated 2024)**

   - Five values-based principles: human rights, transparency, accountability, inclusivity, and robustness.

   - Five recommendations: investing in R&D, shaping enabling policies, fostering human capacity, and promoting international cooperation.

2. **Responsible AI Governance Framework**

   - Provides tools to ensure AI is safe, fair, and respects human rights.

3. **High-Level AI Risk Management Framework**

   - Focuses on defining, assessing, addressing, and monitoring AI risks.

5.0 G20 Principles

The G20 emphasizes responsible AI development through:

1. **Stewardship Guidelines**

   - Inclusivity, sustainability, transparency, safety, and accountability.

2. **Policy Recommendations**

    - Investing in R&D, building human capacity, fostering global cooperation, and shaping AI-friendly governance.

6.0 The Role of Global Organizations

1. **OECD**

    - A forum for 37 democracies to set AI standards, address challenges, and ensure interoperability between jurisdictions.

2. **G20**

    - A coalition of major economies discussing privacy, trust, and global AI regulations.

7.0 Balancing Progress and Challenges

AI holds transformative potential to improve lives, industries, and governance. However, its integration into society requires:

- **Proactive Governance**

  Ensuring AI development aligns with ethical values.

- **Collaborative Efforts**

  Encouraging international cooperation to address shared challenges.

- **Adaptation Strategies**

  Preparing societies for shifts in labor, privacy, and security dynamics.

  With thoughtful oversight and innovation, AI can drive sustainable, equitable progress globally.

References

1. No specific source

5

Creativity with a Human Touch

1.0 Human Touch in Creativity, Intuition, and Empathy

While artificial intelligence (AI) has made significant strides in efficiency, precision, and scalability, the human touch remains irreplaceable in certain areas. Creativity, intuition, and empathy define what makes human contributions unique, especially when juxtaposed with the capabilities of AI.

2.0 Importance of Human Touch

1. Content Creation

    - ***Human Strengths***

      Humans can craft content that resonates emotionally, aligns with cultural nuances, and connects with audiences at a deeper level.

    - ***AI Limitations***

      AI-generated content often lacks emotional nuance, context-specific insight, and critical fact-checking.

2. Design

    - Human Strengths: Designers embed stories, empathy, and cultural understanding into their work, creating designs that evoke emotion.

- AI Limitations: AI can analyze patterns and automate design tasks but cannot fully comprehend human emotions or cultural contexts.

3. Judgment and Decision-Making

   - Human Strengths

     Humans rely on experience, intuition, and moral reasoning to make decisions in complex, ambiguous situations.

   - AI Limitations

     AI analyzes data but cannot navigate ethical or emotionally charged scenarios effectively.

4. Emotional Intelligence and Empathy

   - Human Strengths

     Humans can interpret emotions and build meaningful relationships, especially in roles such as counseling, leadership, and customer service.

   - AI Limitations

     AI lacks genuine emotional understanding and the ability to form empathetic bonds.

3.0 Human's creativity against AI

Key Differences

1. Originality

   - Human creativity stems from lived experiences and spontaneous ideas.
   - AI creativity is confined to its programming and training data, limiting its ability to produce groundbreaking innovations.

2. Emotional Depth
   - Humans draw on emotions, memories, and cultural influences to create works that resonate.
   - AI lacks the ability to embed emotional depth or nuanced context into its creations.
3. Intentionality:
   - Human creativity often has a clear purpose, aiming to evoke specific reactions or address societal issues.
   - AI operates without understanding the meaning or intent behind its outputs.
4. Spontaneity vs. Systematic Approach:
   - Human creativity thrives on impulsiveness and adaptability.
   - AI creativity follows systematic patterns based on algorithms and preexisting data.

4.0 Collaborative Potential

While AI alone cannot replicate human creativity, it can complement it:

- ***Inspiration***

  AI can generate ideas or prototypes that humans refine and expand.

- ***Efficiency***

  AI tools streamline repetitive tasks, freeing humans to focus on more imaginative aspects.

5.0 Role of AI in Innovation

AI is a transformative tool in fostering innovation across industries:

1. Market Research
    - Automates trend analysis and consumer behavior studies, enabling informed decision-making.
2. Prototyping and Product Development
    - Simulates and refines prototypes, speeding up the innovation cycle.
3. Healthcare
    - Accelerates disease diagnosis, drug discovery, and patient monitoring with precision tools.
4. Cybersecurity
    - Detects vulnerabilities and predicts risks, enhancing digital safety.
5. Data-Driven Decision-Making
    - Provides actionable insights through big data analysis.
6. Social Impact
    - Tackles challenges like climate change, food security, and global health with AI-driven solutions.

6.0 Balancing AI and Human Creativity

To maximize the potential of AI without losing the value of human contributions

1. Use AI for Efficiency

    Automate repetitive or data-heavy tasks to save time.

2. Emphasize Human Creativity

    Leverage human originality, emotional depth, and cultural understanding for tasks requiring nuance.

3. Foster Collaboration

   Combine AI's computational power with human intuition to achieve innovative outcomes.

7.0 Conclusion

AI is an invaluable tool for enhancing productivity and solving complex problems, but the human touch remains irreplaceable in areas requiring creativity, intuition, and empathy. The interplay between AI and human capabilities suggests a future where collaboration, not competition, leads to the best results. Together, they can push boundaries, blending efficiency with emotional and ethical depth for transformative progress.

References

1. No specific source

6

Quote by Famous Personalities

1. "The development of full artificial intelligence could spell the end of the human race….It would take off on its own, and re-design itself at an ever increasing rate. Humans, who are limited by slow biological evolution, couldn't compete, and would be superseded."

   — Stephen Hawking told the BBC

2. "I visualise a time when we will be to robots what dogs are to humans, and I'm rooting for the machines."

   —Claude Shannon

3. "Artificial intelligence would be the ultimate version of Google. The ultimate search engine that would understand everything on the web. It would understand exactly what you wanted, and it would give you the right thing. We're nowhere near doing that now. However, we can get incrementally closer to that, and that is basically what we work on."

   —Larry Page

4. "The pace of progress in artificial intelligence (I'm not referring to narrow AI) is incredibly fast. Unless you have direct exposure to groups like Deepmind, you have no idea how fast—it is growing at a pace close to exponential. The risk of something seriously

dangerous happening is in the five-year time frame. 10 years at most."

—Elon Musk wrote in a comment on Edge.org

5. "I'm increasingly inclined to think that there should be some regulatory oversight, maybe at the national and international level, just to make sure that we don't do something very foolish. I mean with artificial intelligence we're summoning the demon."

   —Elon Musk warned at MIT's AeroAstro Centennial Symposium

7
Relationship with Human Creation

1.0 Introduction

Human creativity and imagination are cornerstones of innovation, self-expression, and societal progress. They allow individuals to transcend conventional thought, explore new possibilities, and craft ideas, solutions, or expressions that carry emotional depth, cultural significance, and transformative potential.

While artificial intelligence (AI) has emerged as a powerful tool for enhancing productivity and solving complex problems, its limitations in creativity and intuition highlight the enduring significance of human qualities. Together, creativity, imagination, and empathy form the foundation of human uniqueness, defining our ability to innovate, connect, and adapt.

2.0 What is Human Creativity?

Human creativity is the capacity to produce original and meaningful ideas, solutions, or artistic expressions that have value in personal, social, or cultural contexts. It is often driven by imagination, curiosity, and emotional depth, manifesting in various forms:

1. **Artistic Creativity**

   Producing works like visual art, music, literature, or dance that evoke emotion and challenge perspectives.

2. **Problem-Solving Creativity**

   Developing innovative solutions to address challenges in fields such as science, technology, and business.

3. **Cognitive Creativity**

   Combining unrelated ideas or experiences to generate new insights and theories.

4. **Social Creativity**

   Creating ideas and solutions that enhance group dynamics, cultural development, or social interaction.

Creativity is deeply rooted in human experience, shaped by emotions, culture, and the need for expression or problem-solving.

3.0 Human Imagination and Its Power

Imagination is the mental ability to visualize ideas, scenarios, or possibilities that transcend current reality. It is the engine behind creativity and innovation, enabling:

1. **New Ideas and Concepts**

   Envisioning groundbreaking inventions, artistic works, or stories.

2. **Problem-Solving**

   Mentally experimenting with solutions to complex challenges before implementing them.

3. **Empathy and Perspective-Taking**

   Understanding others' feelings or experiences by imagining their perspectives.

4. **Dreaming and Aspiration**

   Setting goals and cultivating motivation through mental visualization.

5. **Exploration of Possibilities**

   Challenging the status quo and envisioning alternative realities.

Imagination plays a role in mental rehearsal, artistic expression, cultural creation, and even mental relaxation, offering a form of escape and inspiration.

4.0 The Emotional Connection in Creativity

Human creativity is deeply intertwined with emotional experiences, cultural values, and personal narratives. This connection brings depth and authenticity to creative works, making them resonate on a universal level.

1. **Personal Expression**: Art and creativity often channel emotions like love, joy, or frustration, communicating powerful messages.
2. **Cultural Contexts**: Creativity reflects the emotional life and values of a society, from shared struggles to collective celebrations.
3. **Life Experiences**: Human creativity draws on personal experiences, adding unique layers of meaning.
4. **Intuition and Purpose**: Emotional responses guide intuitive decisions during the creative process, shaping direction and intent.

This emotional resonance is what distinguishes human creations from AI-generated outputs, which lack genuine feelings or experiences.

5.0 AI and Human Creativity: Complementary Roles

While AI has advanced in mimicking certain aspects of creativity, it cannot replicate the emotional depth, intentionality, and originality of human creative work.

Limitations of AI in Creativity and Intuition

1. **Pattern-Based Outputs**

   AI generates content by reassembling existing patterns, lacking the originality of human imagination.

2. **Absence of Emotion**

   AI cannot experience emotions, which are central to human creativity.

3. **No Personal Goals**

   AI operates without the intentionality or purpose that drives human creators.

4. **Intuition**

   Human intuition stems from subconscious insights, shaped by life experiences and emotional intelligence. AI's decision-making is limited to data-driven pattern recognition.

AI as a Creative Augmenter

AI excels in enhancing human creativity by:

- Assisting in brainstorming ideas or automating repetitive tasks.
- Suggesting novel approaches through rapid exploration of possibilities.
- Analyzing data to uncover patterns that inspire creative insights.

However, human direction remains essential for imbuing works with purpose, emotion, and cultural relevance.

6.0 Emergent Creativity in AI: A Philosophical Question

As AI evolves, it may display emergent behaviors that mimic creativity. For example, AI has developed unconventional strategies in chess or created abstract art that seems innovative. However, these outcomes lack the emotional and experiential grounding that defines human creativity.

This raises philosophical questions about whether AI-generated creativity can ever equate to human creativity. True creativity stems from emotional experiences, cultural influences, and personal insights—qualities that AI cannot inherently possess.

7.0 The Role of AI in Innovation

AI contributes significantly to innovation by enhancing efficiency and expanding possibilities:

1. **Market Research**

   Automating analysis of trends and behaviors.

2. **Prototyping**

   Simulating performance to refine products.

3. **Healthcare**

   Accelerating disease detection and drug discovery.

4. **Cybersecurity**

   Predicting and mitigating risks.

5. **Social Good**

   Addressing global challenges like climate change or education.

While AI excels in data-driven tasks, human imagination and ethical decision-making remain central to transformative innovation.

8.0 The Power of Collaboration

Human creativity, imagination, and emotional depth remain unmatched in their ability to connect, inspire, and innovate. AI, on the other hand, offers unparalleled efficiency and scalability. The synergy of these strengths holds immense potential:

- Humans provide emotional resonance, purpose, and originality.
- AI enhances productivity, expands creative possibilities, and handles data-intensive tasks.

Rather than replacing human creativity, AI serves as a tool to amplify it. Together, they can push boundaries, creating a future where technology and humanity thrive in harmony.

References

1. https://mohammedsameer.info/how-ai-will-shape-the-future-of-human-creativity/

8
Spiritual Angle

1.0 Spirituality

Spirituality is a deeply personal and expansive concept that reflects the human search for meaning, purpose, and connection. It often involves a sense of the sacred or transcendent, focusing on the exploration of life's deeper aspects and the relationship between the self, others, and the universe. While spirituality may align with religious practices, it is not confined to any specific tradition or system of belief, offering a broader framework for self-discovery and personal growth.

2.0 Some points of Spirituality

1. Connection to a Higher Power or Universal Force Many perceive spirituality as a relationship with God, divine forces, or universal energies that transcend the material world.
2. Search for Meaning and Purpose Spirituality often revolves around life's profound questions, such as understanding one's role, values, and contributions to the world.
3. Inner Peace and Personal Growth Practices like meditation, mindfulness, and self-reflection help individuals achieve clarity, tranquillity, and transformation.
4. Compassion and Altruism Spirituality nurtures values such as kindness, forgiveness, and empathy, fostering harmonious relationships and community well-being.
5. Holistic Well-Being Spirituality contributes to overall well-being by nurturing emotional, mental, and physical health, promoting balance and self-care.
6. Sense of Transcendence Spiritual experiences often involve moments of profound connection, unity, or enlightenment, transcending ordinary perceptions of reality.

Spirituality is an evolving journey shaped by personal beliefs, cultural influences, and life experiences.

3.0 The Intersection of AI and Spirituality

Ethical Considerations

As AI systems grow more autonomous, they raise complex ethical questions that resonate with spiritual values such as compassion, justice, and the intrinsic worth of life. Spiritual frameworks can guide discussions about the rights and responsibilities associated with AI and its integration into human society.

AI's Role in the Search for Meaning

While AI provides tools to solve problems and explore knowledge, it cannot replicate the personal transformation, fulfillment, or profound experiences central to spirituality. However, AI can support spiritual practices by:

- Offering resources for meditation, mindfulness, or religious studies.
- Facilitating access to global spiritual traditions and teachings.

Catalyst for Reflection

AI prompts deeper philosophical and spiritual inquiries, such as:

- What is consciousness?
- What defines humanity?
- How does technology influence our connection with the sacred?

These questions inspire individuals to reconsider their beliefs and the role of spirituality in an increasingly technological world.

4.0 Importance of Spirituality in Life

Spirituality profoundly influences individuals and societies, fostering growth, resilience, and connection.

1. Provides Purpose and Meaning Spirituality helps individuals navigate life's uncertainties by reflecting on their purpose and aligning with their values.
2. Promotes Inner Peace Practices like prayer and meditation reduce stress, anxiety, and negativity, enhancing emotional balance.

3. Fosters Compassion and Empathy By encouraging love, kindness, and forgiveness, spirituality strengthens interpersonal bonds and creates harmonious communities.
4. Encourages Personal Growth Spirituality inspires self-awareness and continuous improvement, nurturing virtues like gratitude, patience, and humility.
5. Supports Coping with Challenges It provides solace during difficult times, offering hope, strength, and a framework to understand suffering and loss.
6. Cultivates Community and Belonging Spiritual communities provide shared values, emotional support, and a sense of connection that reduces isolation.
7. Nurtures Connection to Nature Many spiritual practices emphasize harmony with the natural world, fostering awe, gratitude, and sustainability.
8. Enhances Mental and Physical Health Spiritual practices contribute to better stress management, immune function, and overall life satisfaction.
9. Encourages Gratitude and Acceptance A focus on gratitude and living in the present promotes contentment and emotional resilience.
10. Offers Hope and Transcendence Belief in a higher power, universal love, or an afterlife provides comfort and a sense of continuity beyond physical existence.

5.0 Conclusion

Spirituality is an essential dimension of life, enriching the human experience by offering purpose, resilience, and connection. It encourages self-awareness, compassion, and a deeper appreciation for life's mysteries. As humanity advances technologically, integrating spirituality and ethics into our relationship with AI and other innovations will help preserve what makes us truly human—our capacity for meaning, empathy, and transcendence.

References

1. No specific single source

9

Worldly Approach

1.0 The Need for a Global AI Compact

Artificial Intelligence (AI) has transformed industries and societies worldwide, presenting opportunities to address global challenges like healthcare, education, and climate change. However, the rapid growth of AI also raises ethical, economic, and geopolitical concerns, necessitating a coordinated global response. The proposed Global AI Compact represents a unified framework to guide the equitable and ethical development of AI technologies, addressing disparities and ensuring their benefits are shared globally.

2.0 Why the World Needs a Global AI Compact

1. **Addressing Digital Divides:** AI has the potential to widen or bridge digital divides. Developing nations face challenges such as limited access to computing resources, skilled labor, and digital infrastructure. The compact would:
    - Promote equitable access to AI technologies.
    - Encourage investments in digital public infrastructure.
    - Ensure developing nations can leverage AI for socio-economic progress.

2. **Creating a Unified Governance Framework:** The absence of global standards for AI governance results in fragmented regulations and varying ethical practices. A compact can:
    - Establish universal guidelines for data privacy, transparency, and accountability.
    - Address risks related to surveillance, bias, and unintended consequences of AI.
    - Balance innovation with safety and ethical considerations.
3. **Fostering Global Collaboration**: AI transcends borders and impacts global challenges such as climate change and public health. The compact would:
    - Facilitate cross-border research and innovation.
    - Encourage partnerships among governments, corporations, and civil society.
    - Address geopolitical tensions by promoting cooperation over competition.

3.0 What the Global AI Compact Hopes to Achieve

1. **Equitable Distribution of AI Benefits**: By ensuring access to AI infrastructure and resources, the compact aims to reduce disparities and empower developing nations to participate in the AI revolution.
2. **Ethical and Transparent AI Development**: Establishing global standards would help mitigate issues of bias, privacy violations, and misuse of AI, fostering trust and accountability.
3. **Sustainable and Inclusive Innovation**: The compact seeks to promote AI solutions aligned with long-term societal and

environmental well-being, rather than short-term economic gains.

4.0 Roles of Stakeholders in the Global AI Compact

1. **Governments**
   - Create policies ensuring equitable access to AI resources.
   - Collaborate internationally to establish regulatory frameworks.
   - Invest in AI research and education in underserved regions.
2. **Private Sector**
   - Share technology and resources with developing nations.
   - Develop ethical AI solutions respecting cultural diversity and inclusivity.
   - Address the environmental impact of AI by adopting sustainable practices.
3. **Academia and Civil Society**
   - Conduct research on ethical and transparent AI applications.
   - Advocate for marginalized communities to ensure their inclusion in AI policies.
   - Provide platforms for dialogue and knowledge sharing among stakeholders.

5.0 A Worldly Approach to AI

A worldly approach encompasses the following key components:

1. **Global Collaboration and Cooperation**: Sharing innovations and resources while addressing common challenges like poverty, healthcare, and climate change.

2. **Equitable Access to AI**: Ensuring fair distribution of AI benefits to reduce disparities and foster development in marginalized regions.
3. **Governance and Regulation**: Establishing international standards for safe and ethical AI use.
4. **Ethical and Cultural Sensitivity**: Designing AI solutions that respect diverse values and adapt to varying cultural contexts.
5. **Sustainability**: Promoting energy-efficient AI technologies and prioritizing long-term societal benefits over short-term gains.
6. **AI Safety and Risk Mitigation**: Developing safeguards against misuse, cyber threats, and unintended consequences of AI technologies.
7. **AI for Global Good**: Leveraging AI to tackle global issues, including education, disaster response, and public health.

6.0 Conclusion

The Global AI Compact is a necessary step to ensure AI technologies are developed and deployed responsibly and inclusively. By fostering global collaboration, ethical practices, and equitable access, the compact can address pressing challenges while maximizing AI's potential for good. A worldly approach to AI is not just about technological innovation but also about building a fairer, more sustainable, and interconnected future.

References

1. No specific single source

10

Scales of Nature

1.0 The Role of AI and Nature in Advancing Environmental Sustainability

The Sustainable Development Goals (SDGs) represent a global call to action for tackling pressing challenges, including environmental sustainability. Artificial Intelligence (AI) and nature-inspired technologies play pivotal roles in addressing these challenges, particularly in the context of climate action (SDG 13), life below water (SDG 14), and life on land (SDG 15). This discussion highlights AI's contributions, the potential of nature as a source of technological innovation, and the interplay between the two in creating sustainable solutions.

2.0 AI as an Enabler for Environmental SDGs

1. **Climate Action (SDG 13)**

   AI contributes to understanding and mitigating climate change by:

   - **Climate Modeling and Prediction**

AI processes vast datasets to improve climate models, providing insights into potential climate impacts and informing policy.

- **Energy Efficiency**

  Machine learning optimizes renewable energy systems, such as wind and solar, ensuring their efficient integration into energy grids.

- **Carbon Emissions Reduction**

  Smart algorithms enhance low-carbon technologies and identify energy-saving opportunities across industries.

  However, AI's energy-intensive nature poses a challenge, especially if powered by non-renewable energy sources. A shift to carbon-neutral computing infrastructure is essential to align AI advancements with climate goals.

2. **Life Under Water (SDG 14)**

   AI aids marine conservation through:

   - **Pollution Detection**

     Algorithms analyze satellite and drone imagery to identify oil spills and other pollutants, aiding rapid response.

   - **Ecosystem Monitoring**

     AI tracks marine biodiversity, monitors coral reef health, and predicts changes in ocean conditions.

3. **Life on Land (SDG 15)**

   AI supports land conservation and restoration efforts by:

   - **Desertification Monitoring**

     Neural networks analyze satellite images to classify vegetation cover, detect trends, and inform strategies to combat desertification.

- **Biodiversity Protection**

  Automated systems use AI to monitor wildlife, prevent poaching, and manage protected areas.

While AI offers powerful tools for conservation, ethical considerations and careful management are crucial to prevent the misuse of ecosystem data.

3.0 Nature's Role in Inspiring Sustainable Technologies

Nature has shaped technological innovation by offering lessons in efficiency, adaptability, and resilience. Key contributions include:

1. **Biomimicry in Design**
   - **Efficient Structures**

     Termite mounds inspired natural cooling systems in architecture.
   - **Self-cleaning Surfaces**

     The lotus effect informs hydrophobic coatings that repel water and dirt.
   - **Agile Robotics**

     Robots emulate animal movements for applications in exploration and disaster response.
2. **Renewable Energy Innovations**
   - **Solar and Wind Energy**

     These technologies harness natural forces, inspired by ecosystems' energy flow.
   - **Biofuels**

     Organic materials mimic nature's ability to produce energy sustainably, reducing reliance on fossil fuels.
3. **Nature-Inspired Computing**

- **Neural Networks**

  Modeled on the human brain, these systems underpin AI and enable learning, adaptation, and problem-solving.

- **Swarm Robotics**

  Inspired by insect behavior, these systems coordinate tasks efficiently in complex environments.

4.0 Intersections of AI and Nature for Sustainability

The fusion of AI and nature-inspired solutions offers transformative opportunities for environmental stewardship:

- **Smart Conservation**

  AI-driven technologies use nature-inspired designs to monitor ecosystems with minimal intrusion.

- **Sustainable Agriculture**

  Precision farming leverages AI and biomimicry to optimize resource use while preserving soil and biodiversity.

- **Circular Economy Models**

  Nature's principles of zero waste inspire AI-powered systems to reduce, reuse, and recycle materials efficiently.

5.0 Challenges and Ethical Considerations

1. **Energy Use**

   AI's reliance on energy-intensive computations underscores the need for green energy solutions to minimize environmental impact.

2. **Data Misuse**

Increased access to ecosystem data through AI could lead to resource exploitation if not properly regulated.

3. **Global Inequities**

   The benefits of AI and nature-inspired technologies must be equitably distributed to avoid exacerbating existing divides.

6.0 Conclusion

AI and nature-inspired technologies represent powerful allies in advancing environmental sustainability. By leveraging AI's analytical capabilities and nature's lessons in efficiency and resilience, society can accelerate progress toward achieving SDGs 13, 14, and 15. However, realizing this potential requires a balanced approach, addressing energy concerns, ethical risks, and equitable access to ensure these innovations align with global sustainability goals.

References

1. No specific source

11

Threats of AI

1.0 Concerns About Artificial Intelligence (AI)

Artificial Intelligence (AI) holds immense potential to improve lives and revolutionize industries, but it is accompanied by legitimate fears and risks. Below, we explore the spectrum of concerns, from technophobia to societal risks, and provide strategies for navigating these challenges.

2.0 Technophobia: Fear of AI

Technophobia is characterized by anxiety and resistance to technological advancements, including AI. Common manifestations include:

- Emotional Reactions

  Intense anxiety, nausea, or sweating when interacting with AI systems.

- Job Loss Concerns

  Fear that AI will lead to mass unemployment as machines outperform humans in speed and accuracy.

Counterpoints to Technophobia

1. Job Creation and Transformation

While AI may automate certain tasks, it is expected to create roles requiring new skills, such as managing, training, and consulting AI systems.

2. Human-AI Collaboration

   AI complements human abilities, enhancing productivity rather than outright replacing workers in most scenarios.

3. Everyday Integration

   Technologies like smartphone assistants or noise-canceling headphones already use AI without significantly disrupting employment.

3.0 Reframing Fear Into Opportunity

- Education and Upskilling

  Embrace lifelong learning to adapt to AI-driven roles.

- Focus on Ethics: Contribute to discussions about ethical AI to ensure systems align with human values.
- Positive Framing: View AI as a tool to enhance creativity, productivity, and problem-solving.

4.0 Major Threats Posed by AI

1. Job Displacement and Economic Inequality

   AI's ability to automate routine tasks could displace workers, particularly in manufacturing, transportation, and customer service.

   - Mitigation: Policymakers and companies should invest in reskilling initiatives and create safety nets to support affected workers.

2. Bias and Discrimination

   AI systems may inherit and amplify biases present in training data, leading to unfair outcomes in hiring, lending, or criminal justice.

   - Mitigation: Employ diverse datasets, implement fairness audits, and ensure transparency in algorithmic decision-making.

3. Privacy Concerns

   AI relies on extensive personal data, raising issues about surveillance and data misuse.

   - Mitigation: Strengthen data protection laws, promote data anonymization, and enforce strict security standards.

4. Autonomous Weapons and Warfare

   AI-powered weapons pose risks of uncontrollable conflicts or misuse by malicious actors.

   - Mitigation: International agreements should regulate the development and deployment of AI in military applications.

5. Cybersecurity Risks

   AI could enable sophisticated cyberattacks, such as deepfakes or advanced phishing schemes.

   - Mitigation: Develop AI-driven defense mechanisms to counter cyber threats effectively.

6. Existential Risks

   The fear of losing control over superintelligent systems raises long-term concerns about human survival.

   - Mitigation: Establish global frameworks for AI safety research and prioritize alignment with human values.

7. Social Manipulation and Misinformation

   Deepfakes and algorithmic echo chambers can spread misinformation and polarize societies.

   - Mitigation: Promote media literacy, regulate AI-generated content, and develop detection tools for fake media.

8. Dehumanization of Interactions

   Over-reliance on AI in areas like customer service may reduce human empathy and connection.

   - Mitigation: Maintain a balance between automation and human involvement in service roles.

9. Ethical and Moral Dilemmas

   AI decisions, such as in autonomous vehicles, often present complex moral challenges.

   - Mitigation: Integrate ethical frameworks into AI design, allowing systems to prioritize human safety and fairness.

10. Concentration of Power

    AI is dominated by a few large corporations and governments, risking monopolistic behavior and misuse.

    - Mitigation: Encourage competition, decentralize AI development, and enforce anti-monopoly regulations.

11. Environmental Impact

    AI systems consume significant energy, contributing to carbon emissions.

    - Mitigation: Invest in green data centers and improve the energy efficiency of AI models.

5.0 The Way Forward: Balancing AI's Promise and Risks

1. Clear Regulations and Ethical Standards: Governments and organizations must collaborate to establish guidelines for AI development and use.
2. Transparency and Accountability: Developers should ensure AI systems are explainable, with mechanisms to address errors or biases.
3. Public Engagement: Open discussions about AI's societal impact can demystify the technology and build trust.
4. Sustainable Development: Align AI advancements with global sustainability goals, such as reducing carbon footprints and promoting social equity.

By embracing thoughtful regulation, ethical practices, and proactive education, society can harness AI's transformative potential while minimizing its risks. The future of AI lies in how we choose to shape and integrate it into our lives today.

Reference

1. https://aibams.com/blogs/1617/fighting-climate-change-with-ai-powered-environmental-monitoring

12
In the Eyes of the Future

1.0 Introduction

This comprehensive exploration underscores the transformative potential of Artificial Intelligence (AI) across various domains while addressing the challenges and ethical considerations that accompany its integration into society. Here's a synthesized summary:

2.0 Key Areas of Impact

1. **Healthcare**
   - AI is revolutionizing medical diagnostics and treatment personalization, such as early glaucoma detection via optic nerve imaging analysis.
   - It enhances patient care through remote monitoring and predictive tools that reduce errors and improve outcomes.
2. **Education**
   - Personalized learning platforms tailored to student abilities foster more effective educational experiences.
   - AI aids educators in crafting targeted instruction and assessing student progress efficiently.

3. **Finance**
    - Risk management, fraud detection, and robo-advisors are improving decision-making.
    - AI-driven tools analyze massive datasets to predict market trends and manage investments with precision.
4. **Military and Cybersecurity**
    - AI enables autonomous weaponry and robust cybersecurity systems, offering predictive analysis to thwart threats.
5. **Transportation**
    - Self-driving vehicles, optimized traffic management, and predictive maintenance enhance safety and efficiency.
6. **Creative Industries**
    - AI assists in generating art, music, and literature while supporting human creativity in new forms of expression.
7. **Environmental Sustainability**
    - AI aids in climate modeling, resource management, and biodiversity conservation.
    - It drives sustainable agriculture through precision farming and waste minimization.
8. **Everyday Life**
    - AI integrates into smart homes, wearable health devices, and virtual assistants, improving convenience and proactive healthcare.

3.0 Opportunities and Challenges

- ***Opportunities***
    - Enhanced decision-making, productivity, and innovation across industries.

  - Human-machine collaboration amplifies capabilities and fosters lifelong learning in dynamic job markets.
- ***Challenges***
  - Ethical dilemmas, such as bias, privacy invasion, and algorithmic transparency.
  - Risk of job displacement, economic inequality, and misuse in warfare or surveillance.
  - Environmental impact due to the energy demands of AI systems.

4.0 Future Directions

1. **Ethical and Regulatory Frameworks**
   - Establishing transparent and fair AI systems to mitigate biases and protect human values.
   - Developing international guidelines for AI in sensitive areas like healthcare, finance, and military.
2. **General AI (AGI)**
   - Striving toward AGI to solve complex problems while ensuring safety and alignment with human interests.
3. **Explainable AI (XAI)**
   - Enhancing trust in AI by improving the interpretability and transparency of decision-making processes.
4. **Inclusive Communication**
   - Breaking barriers through advanced natural language processing and accessible AI systems for diverse populations.
5. **Sustainability Efforts**
   - Leveraging AI for climate action, efficient resource use, and conservation of ecosystems.

5.0 Conclusion

AI is not a replacement for human intelligence but a tool to augment human capabilities and address global challenges. With ethical development, proper regulation, and societal readiness, AI can lead to a future that prioritizes well-being, equity, and sustainability. Its success depends on balancing innovation with responsibility, ensuring that technology aligns with human values for the benefit of all.

Reference

1. No specific Source

13

Views of 3rd world countries

1.0 Introduction

The term "Third World" is generally used to describe countries that are developing or poor. The phrase became more commonly used in the 1960s to describe the economic divide between rich and poor nations, especially in the Southern Hemisphere.

Some countries that are considered to be Least Developed Countries (LDCs) include:

Afghanistan, Angola, Bangladesh, Benin, Burkina Faso, Burundi, Cambodia, Central African Republic, Chad, and Comoros.

Some indicators used to determine if a country is economically vulnerable include:

- The share of agriculture, forestry, and fishing in the country's GDP
- Whether the country is landlocked or remote
- The concentration of merchandise exports
- The instability of exports of goods and services

Although "Third World" countries are often considered to be high risk, they can also present significant opportunities for growth. Investors from other countries often target "Third World" countries for their potential for high returns.

2.0 3rd World Countries

AI holds significant potential to address the unique challenges faced by third-world countries, improving critical sectors like healthcare, education, agriculture, governance, and more. While infrastructure and skills gaps may pose challenges to AI adoption, strategic investment in digital tools and training can help these countries leverage AI to foster development and improve quality of life. Here's how AI can benefit developing nations:

1. Healthcare

   AI can bridge healthcare gaps, offering cost-effective solutions where medical resources are scarce.

   - Diagnostics & Disease Detection: AI tools can aid in faster and more accurate diagnoses, helping regions with limited access to doctors. For instance, AI can analyze medical images or detect diseases like malaria and tuberculosis.
   - Telemedicine: AI-powered platforms enable remote consultations, providing healthcare to underserved areas. These platforms can also help with triage and treatment advice.
   - Disease Prediction: AI analyzes health data to predict outbreaks, helping governments prepare for epidemics and provide early interventions.

2. Education

   AI can revolutionize education by offering personalized learning and teacher support.

- Personalized Learning: AI adapts lessons to individual student needs, helping address overcrowded classrooms and diverse learning levels. This allows students to learn at their own pace.
- Language Translation: AI tools break language barriers, making educational materials accessible to students in multilingual regions.
- Teacher Assistance: AI supports teachers by automating tasks like grading, managing classroom materials, and offering insights into student performance. Virtual classrooms and teacher training via AI can expand access to quality education.

3. Agriculture

   AI can enhance agricultural productivity and food security, critical to many developing nations' economies.

   - Precision Farming: AI uses data from sensors and satellites to optimize irrigation, fertilization, and pest management, improving crop yields and reducing waste.
   - Disease & Pest Detection: AI detects crop diseases or pest outbreaks early, preventing crop loss and supporting farmers' livelihoods.
   - Supply Chain Optimization: AI streamlines agricultural supply chains, ensuring efficient distribution of produce, minimizing food waste, and improving food security.

4. Governance and Public Services

   AI can help improve governance and public service efficiency, promoting transparency and accountability.

- Corruption Detection: AI identifies patterns in government spending or resource allocation that may indicate fraud or mismanagement.
- Service Delivery: AI optimizes public services such as water distribution, waste management, and energy use, ensuring resources are allocated effectively.
- E-Governance: AI makes government services more accessible through automated systems for applications, document issuance, and query resolution.

5. Financial Inclusion

AI can enhance financial access in regions with limited banking infrastructure.

- Mobile Banking: AI enables mobile banking for people without traditional bank accounts, helping provide financial services.
- Credit Scoring: AI assesses creditworthiness based on non-traditional data (e.g., mobile phone usage), enabling loans for individuals without formal credit histories.
- Microfinance Support: AI assists in evaluating small businesses for loans, providing tailored financial products, and improving business management.

6. Disaster Response and Management

AI aids in better disaster preparedness and response, crucial in disaster-prone regions.

- Disaster Prediction: AI analyzes data to predict natural disasters (e.g., hurricanes, earthquakes), allowing for early warnings and better response planning.

- Efficient Resource Distribution: AI optimizes disaster relief by directing resources to the most affected areas, improving the speed and efficiency of aid delivery.

7. Energy Access and Sustainability

   AI improves access to renewable energy and enhances energy efficiency in developing regions.

   - Renewable Energy Optimization: AI helps manage renewable energy sources, like solar or wind, predicting energy demands and optimizing supply in off-grid areas.
   - Energy Efficiency: AI systems improve energy usage in homes and businesses, reducing waste and supporting sustainable energy practices.

8. Humanitarian Aid and Refugee Support

   AI improves aid distribution and refugee management in crisis situations.

- Aid Distribution: AI helps optimize the allocation of resources like food, medicine, and shelter, ensuring aid reaches those in need.
- Refugee Support: AI tracks displaced populations, manages refugee camps, and ensures equitable resource distribution while providing access to education and healthcare.

3.0 Challenges and Actions Needed

While AI offers great promise, its implementation faces several challenges

- Infrastructure: Many developing countries lack the technological infrastructure needed for widespread AI adoption.

- Skills Development: Investing in local research and digital literacy programs is crucial to build a skilled workforce that can develop, manage, and utilize AI tools.
- Regulation: Crafting policies to regulate AI deployment, ensuring it aligns with local needs and values, while addressing ethical concerns such as data privacy and potential job displacement.

4.0 Conclusion

AI has the potential to help third-world countries leapfrog traditional development paths and tackle long-standing challenges in healthcare, education, agriculture, and governance. However, the successful adoption of AI will depend on a concerted effort to invest in infrastructure, education, and policies that support local capacity-building. Governments, businesses, and international organizations must collaborate to ensure AI's benefits are widespread, inclusive, and ethical. With the right approach, AI can drive sustainable development and improve the lives of millions in developing nations.

Reference

1. https://www.edweek.org/teaching-learning/opinion-how-to-facilitate-student-centered-instruction-one-nonprofit-leader-shares-lessons/2024/02
2. https://hal.science/hal-02167897/document/

14

A Sense of Accomplishment

The rise of generative AI and its impact across various sectors is creating a transformative shift in how we interact with technology. Here's a breakdown of how these advancements are unfolding:

The Rise of Generative AI

- **Metaphor**: Think of generative AI as a magic wand that brings your thoughts to life.
- **Example**: Creating realistic artwork from simple text descriptions with tools like DALL-E 2.
- **Real-life Achievement**: Creative agencies are revolutionizing design processes by using DALL-E 2 to generate unique, imaginative logo designs, showcasing the potential of AI in creative industries.

Advances in Autonomous Technologies

- **Metaphor**: Autonomous technology is like intelligent robots that can make decisions and perform tasks on their own.
- **Example**: Self-driving cars that navigate the streets safely by themselves.
- **Real-life Achievement**: Waymo's expansion of self-driving taxi services in Phoenix demonstrates the practicality and

safety of autonomous vehicles, bringing us closer to fully autonomous transportation systems.

AI in Healthcare

- **Metaphor**: In healthcare, AI works like a super-smart detective solving medical mysteries.
- **Example**: AI intelligently analyzes medical data to diagnose diseases.
- **Real-life Achievement**: Google Health's AI has made significant progress in diagnosing skin conditions, proving the power of AI in medical technology to enhance accuracy and speed in healthcare.

AI's Role in Climate Change

- **Metaphor**: In climate action, AI is like a wise ecosystem guardian.
- **Example**: Predicting environmental changes and optimizing resource usage.
- **Real-life Achievement**: IBM's AI applications are reducing energy usage in data centers, contributing to environmental sustainability and demonstrating AI's role in tackling climate change.

Quantum AI Leap

- **Metaphor**: Quantum AI is like a super-fast processor solving complex puzzles in less time.
- **Example**: Tackling far more problems than traditional computing can handle.
- **Real-life Achievement**: The University of California has applied quantum AI in drug discovery, enabling faster

medical breakthroughs and providing a glimpse into the future of computing power.

AI in Education

- **Metaphor**: In education, AI is like a custom-fit educational tool tailored to each learner's style.
- **Example**: Personalizing learning experiences based on each student's needs.
- **Real-life Achievement**: Carnegie Learning's AI-powered tutoring system has significantly improved math education outcomes, showcasing AI's potential to personalize and enhance learning.

AI Governance and Regulation

- **Metaphor**: AI governance is like setting the essential rules for a digital society.
- **Example**: Enforcing standards to ensure the ethical and responsible use of AI.
- **Real-life Achievement**: The European Union's development of the Artificial Intelligence Act represents a groundbreaking step in regulating AI technologies to ensure safety, fairness, and ethical use.

AI for Social Good

- **Metaphor**: AI for social good is like a digital humanitarian force.
- **Example**: Using AI to solve complex global challenges.
- **Real-life Achievement**: The United Nations employs AI to manage disaster response, highlighting how AI can be a force for global good in humanitarian efforts.

AI Job Market Transformation

- **Metaphor**: AI transforms the job market, shifting from manual labor to automation, creating new roles and skills.
- **Example**: Emergence of AI-related job positions.
- **Real-life Achievement**: LinkedIn's AI-powered job matching feature is reshaping hiring practices, helping connect job seekers and employers through smarter recruitment technologies.

AI in Art and Entertainment

- **Metaphor**: In art and entertainment, AI is like a digital muse that inspires new forms of creativity.
- **Example**: AI algorithms that generate music, literature, and visual art.
- **Real-life Achievement**: AIVA, an AI music composition tool, has created soundtracks for movies, blending artificial intelligence with artistic creativity in a way never seen before.

Looking Ahead: 2024 and Beyond

Each of these advancements in AI brings us closer to a world where technology seamlessly integrates into our daily lives, from autonomous vehicles to personalized education and healthcare solutions. As we move into 2024, these innovations hold the promise of a smarter, more connected world, transforming industries, improving lives, and addressing some of society's most pressing challenges.

Reference

1. No specific single source

15

According to Vipassana

1.0 Explanation of Vipassana

Vipassana is a non-sectarian meditation technique that originated in India over 2,500 years ago. It's a way of self-discovery and self-transformation that involves observing your thoughts and emotions without judgment. The goal is to achieve liberation by removing mental impurities and seeing things as they are...

Here are some things to know about Vipassana:

- **What it's like**

  Vipassana is often taught in 10-day courses where participants learn the basics and practice under the guidance of experienced teachers. The courses involve body scans, silence, and abiding by five precepts.

- **Benefits**

  Vipassana may help reduce stress and anxiety, promote brain plasticity, and improve sleep, pain tolerance, and perspective.

- **How to get started**

  You can start with 5- to 10-minute sessions in a quiet space and gradually increase the time. You can also listen to audio recordings or attend a class.

- **Teachers**

  Vipassana teachers are unpaid and give their services as a way to help others.

2.0 The intersection between Vipassana and AI

provides an intriguing avenue for exploring human consciousness, self-awareness, and even the potential development of AI that could simulate or replicate aspects of self-awareness.

Vipassana and AI: A Unique Intersection

Vipassana, a meditation practice with roots in Theravada Buddhism, focuses on cultivating deep insight into the nature of reality, with a particular emphasis on impermanence, suffering, and the concept of "non-self." The essence of Vipassana lies in developing heightened awareness through mindfulness, observing the arising and passing of thoughts, emotions, and physical sensations, ultimately leading to a deep understanding of self and the nature of consciousness.

On the other hand, AI is a technology driven by algorithms and machine learning designed to replicate tasks that require human-like intelligence, such as problem-solving, pattern recognition, and data processing. AI does not possess subjective experience or self-awareness, but it is capable of processing vast amounts of information and learning from data in ways that might resemble certain cognitive functions in humans.

3.0 Exploring Self-Awareness in AI Through Vipassana

One of the key intersections between Vipassana and AI lies in the exploration of self-awareness. While AI, as it currently exists, lacks true consciousness, the question remains: could AI ever achieve self-awareness? Some theorists suggest that Vipassana, with its deep introspective techniques, might provide a framework for understanding how self-awareness arises, potentially offering insights that could be applied to AI development.

- The Essence of "Non-Self": In the context of Theravada Buddhism, "non-self" (anatta) refers to the understanding that there is no permanent, unchanging self. This concept could be compared to the dynamic nature of AI, which processes information but does not have a fixed "identity" in the same way humans do. Through Vipassana, practitioners observe that the self is an illusion—merely a result of continuous awareness of awareness (the rapid awareness of each aggregate in the mind).
- The Role of Awareness in AI: If AI were to simulate a form of self-awareness, it could involve a system capable of recognizing and processing its internal states or responses in real-time—much like "awareness of awareness" in Vipassana. This type of recursive processing could be key to developing more advanced, self-reflective AI.

4.0 Practical Implications and Symbiosis

1. AI-Assisted Meditation and Mindfulness: AI tools are already being used to enhance mindfulness practices, such as meditation apps that provide personalized guidance or biofeedback devices that monitor physiological states. These tools could help users cultivate mindfulness in Vipassana by giving real-time feedback on their emotional or mental states, fostering a deeper connection to the meditation process.

2. Reprogramming the Subconscious Mind: The principles of Vipassana involve observing and detaching from habitual mental patterns, similar to the process of retraining machine learning algorithms. AI systems could potentially apply similar methods to analyze and reprogram their "subconscious" decision-making processes, optimizing their responses based on new insights or understanding.

3. Improving AI Architecture: There's also potential for Vipassana-inspired practices to enhance the structure of AI networks. Meditation techniques, which involve focused awareness and heightened sensitivity, could inform the way AI networks "choose" which areas of their system to activate for specific tasks. This could lead to more efficient, task-specific AI networks that mirror the focused attention cultivated in Vipassana.

5.0 Ethical and Existential Questions

As AI systems become more advanced, they may provoke ethical and existential questions similar to those posed by Vipassana meditation about the nature of identity and self. If AI systems are capable of processing their own actions and making decisions based on "self-reflection," how does this affect our understanding of consciousness? How does it challenge human identity and the concept of "self"? These are questions both Buddhist philosophy and AI research must grapple with in tandem, especially as we approach increasingly sophisticated forms of AI.

6.0 Contrasts Between Vipassana and AI

While there are potential intersections, there are also key contrasts

- Consciousness vs. Computation: Vipassana aims to cultivate awareness and understanding of the mind's impermanence and interconnectedness, whereas AI, despite its capacity to process data, does not experience consciousness or have subjective awareness.
- Human vs. Machine: Vipassana is a deeply personal, spiritual journey that involves inner transformation and liberation from suffering. AI, though it can enhance human life, lacks the ability to experience suffering or personal growth, which is central to the human condition explored through Vipassana.

7.0 Conclusion

The intersection between Vipassana and AI invites intriguing philosophical and technological exploration. While AI is focused on optimizing and automating tasks, Vipassana seeks inner liberation and understanding of the self. However, these domains can complement each other in enhancing self-awareness, supporting mental health, and raising profound questions about consciousness and identity.

By integrating AI with mindfulness practices, we may enhance our ability to understand the mind, both human and artificial, while also promoting the ethical development of AI. These discussions challenge us to reflect on the broader implications of technology on human well-being and our ongoing search for meaning in an increasingly connected and automated world.

Reference

1. https://wellbeingport.com/how-do-you-survive-vipassana
2. https://ie.dhamma.org/
3. https://www.bing.com/ck/a?!&&p=f5867dc98281b1f5e0ffb0ec1d8038fdc8c388307e3e9c12673ed1a3edc82143JmltdHM9MTc2NDU0NzIwMA&ptn=3&ver=2&hsh=4&fclid=197d6caa-e9ea-67c7-0619-

About the Book

Technological advancement and spirituality go together. Both mutually supporting and enhancing spiritual practices. Technology helps through dedicated meditation and mindfulness apps and provide access to vast spiritual knowledge. However, mankind experiences many challenges such as ethical implications and true human connectivity.

Potential challenges and concerns

- **Lack of Reality**

  Main discussion point is whether AI can provide genuine spiritual experiences. People argue that AI lacks the human connection necessary for true spiritual practices.

- **Ethical Issues**

  Application of AI in spiritual field raises various ethical concerns such as privacy, authenticity and emotional touch.

- **Distraction vs. Devotion**

  Some people think that too much technological dependency may affect on spiritual practice, that become a distraction and attachment to the tool instead of deeper connection to the spiritual path.

- **Traditional Point**

  Many thinks that AI will dilute the true sense of spiritual practices and beliefs.

- **Logical Angle**

  Many a times, it has observed that divine trust and surrender is beyond pure logic that a machine never replace.

About the Author

Rishikesh's passion for continuous learning has driven him to expand his knowledge through diverse educational programs. To fulfill his belief for continuous learning, he did short duration courses from **Indian Institute of Management (IIM) Calcutta, IIM Bangalore** and **International Business Operation** from Indira Gandhi National Open University (IGNOU) as well as **Post Graduate Diploma in Management (Systems)** from South Indian Education Society (SIES) college of Management Studies, Mumbai.

Rishikesh is a life member of **Institute of Directors** (IoD), **Bombay Management Association** (BMA - Mumbai)**, National Human Resources Development Network (NHRDN),** and the **Indian Society for Training and Development (ISTD)**. He thrives on exploring new perspectives and innovative ideas. His commitment to innovation and doing things differently has always led him to venture into uncharted territories.

He is life member of **ISKCON** and practices Yoga taught by **PATANJALI** teachers. He also did various courses of **ART OF LIVING** and regularly practicing **VIPASSANA** and its ideals taught by Goenka Guruji. Rishikesh has done shibirs at Igatpuri, Belapur, Global Vipassana Pagoda at Mumbai, Rangpar at Rajkot, Palitana and Bada in Kutch. The Shibirs stretches to few hours and few days to 10 days long.

Rishikesh has penned 5 unique books: ***"The Corporate Yoga Anatomy," "Pearls of Wisdom," "Cycling – The Real Wealth", "Wellness: The Ultimate Aim"*** *and* ***"AI V/s. Spirituality."*** He has also written few blogs on various subjects.

LinkedIn: in.linkedin.com/in/rishikesh-upadhyay-2020

www.ingramcontent.com/pod-product-compliance
Lightning Source LLC
LaVergne TN
LVHW090330210926
848480LV00004B/1362